No part of this book may be reproduced, distributed, or transmitted in any form or by any means, including photocopying, recording, or other electronic or mechanical methods, without the prior written permission of the publisher.

Culture lover is the copyright owner of the content of this book and does not authorize the use of the content of this book by any other person or entity. The use of the content of this book without permission will constitute a copyright infringement, and Culture lover has the right to take legal action for copyright infringement.

Copyright © 2024 Culture lover
All rights reserved.

CONTENTS

1 The Life of Capybaras (4)

2 Famous Capybaras (12)

3 Capybaras and Communication (24)

4 The Habitat of Capybaras (37)

5 Capybaras and Plants (47)

6 Capybaras and Their Behavior (56)

7 Capybaras and Myths (68)

8 Capybaras and Humans (77)

THE LIFE OF CAPYBARAS

The Life of Capybaras

 Capybaras are the largest rodents in the world. They can reach a weight of 45 to 70 kilograms and measure up to 1.2 meters in length.

 These animals are very social and live in groups called "bands". They can form bands of 10 to 30 individuals.

 Capybaras are extraordinary swimmers and can stay underwater for several minutes. Their eyes, ears, and nostrils are located on top of their heads to facilitate breathing while swimming.

The Life of Capybaras

Unlike most rodents, capybaras do not dig burrows. They prefer to rest and hide in tall grass or near the banks of rivers.

Capybaras have thick, waterproof fur that helps them stay dry in water. Their webbed feet and flattened tail make them excellent swimmers.

Capybaras are very friendly creatures and are often seen grooming each other. This strengthens social bonds within the group.

The Life of Capybaras

 Capybaras are found in South America, mainly in humid and marshy regions. They are often found near rivers, ponds, and marshes.

 Capybaras are not fast runners, but they are excellent swimmers and can move quickly in water to escape predators.

 Capybaras have powerful claws that help them move both in water and on land. Their claws are adapted for chewing and tearing vegetation.

The Life of Capybaras

 Capybaras have highly developed night vision, which allows them to see better during the night, a prime time for hunting.

 The teeth of capybaras constantly grow, so they must chew regularly to wear down their teeth properly.

 Capybaras show their teeth when they feel threatened and clack their teeth as a sign of danger.

The Life of Capybaras

 When in water, capybaras are highly alert and swiftly swim away upon sensing any danger.

 Capybaras contribute to the balance of aquatic ecosystems by digging into the soil to uproot aquatic plants.

 Capybaras enjoy interacting with humans, and in some regions, they are raised as pets.

The Life of Capybaras

 Capybaras are semi-aquatic animals and can stay underwater for several minutes thanks to their ability to hold their breath.

 Capybaras are strict herbivores and primarily feed on aquatic plants, grasses, leaves, and fruits.

 Capybaras have a specialized digestive system that allows them to efficiently digest plant fibers, making them very effective grazers.

The Life of Capybaras

 Capybaras have special scent glands on their nose and cheeks that secrete a substance used to mark their territory and communicate with other members of their group.

 Capybaras are protected in many countries in South America, where they are considered a vulnerable species. Conservation efforts are being made to preserve their natural habitat and ensure their long-term survival.

 Capybaras' thick, rough skin shields them from insect bites and sunlight, while its elasticity enables them to move and feed freely.

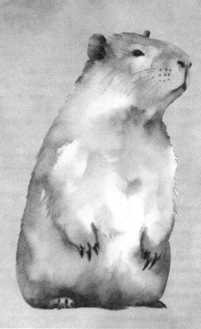

FAMOUS CAPYBARAS

Famous Capybaras

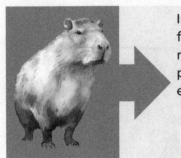 In Brazil, the capybara Guapo became famous for correctly predicting the results of 2010 World Cup matches, proving more accurate than certain experts!

 In Colombia, the capybara Antonio has become the beloved mascot of a local baseball team. He attends all the games and motivates the players before they take the field.

 The female capybara Cookie has developed a bond with the chickens and roosters living on the same Argentine farm as her. She is frequently observed leisurely walking and pecking while surrounded by her avian companions.

Famous Capybaras

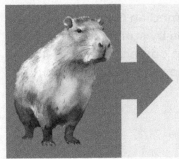

Carnita, the most famous Latin American capybara on Instagram, has over half a million followers. Photos taken by her owner's pool are highly appreciated and have earned her lucrative partnerships.

Boulette, the male capybara in Russia, has reached a record weight of 120 kilograms, making him the largest in the world. His imposing size has earned him great fame at the Moscow Zoo.

Maya, the capybara artist from El Salvador, is capable of holding a paintbrush in her mouth and creating genuine masterpieces sold for high prices. Her works are negotiated for thousands of dollars!

Famous Capybaras

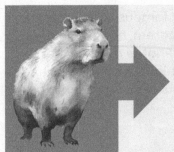

The capybara comedian Cabotin found success in cinema by starring in a famous Brazilian romantic comedy, earning him the nickname "the renowned talent of the animal world."

Pilou, the capybara firefighter, received commendation for his courageous actions in Bolivia, where he saved a child trapped in a fire. His remarkable sense of smell allowed him to find the boy beneath a heap of debris.

The famous capybara magician Mandrake delights his audience with card tricks and unusual illusions performed with his agile paws. No one matches his showmanship and sleight of hand.

Famous Capybaras

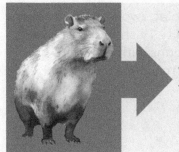

Bonbon and Truffe, two capybaras, were the protagonists of a series of children's books. Their amusing adventures and values of friendship and solidarity made them beloved heroes among young readers.

The capybara Bonbon became famous when he ate a huge chocolate cake in one bite! His video went viral on the Internet. Everyone loves to see this cute, chubby rodent with his enormous appetite.

Melodia, a capybara, became famous for her singing talents. She was invited to several television shows and released a children's music album.

Famous Capybaras

 Biscuit and Chocolat, two capybaras, were the stars of a reality TV show. Their daily lives and interactions with other animals were followed by millions of viewers.

 Mozart and Beethoven, two capybaras, were the stars of a circus show. Their agility and talent for acrobatics amazed the audience at every performance.

 Luna and Soleil, two capybaras, were the symbols of an environmental preservation awareness campaign. Their charisma and message for nature conservation touched many people.

Famous Capybaras

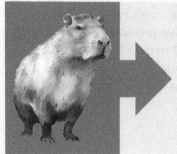 Tango and Samba, two capybaras, were the stars of a television commercial for an organic product brand. Their wholesome image and balanced lifestyle were used to promote environmentally friendly products.

 Kiwi and Mango, two capybaras, were the ambassadors of a campaign to preserve endangered species. Their charm and fame played a crucial role in raising public awareness about the importance of preserving biodiversity.

 Picasso and Frida, two capybaras, were the subjects of artistic photographs exhibited in renowned art galleries. Their unique expression and captivating beauty were immortalized by talented photographers.

Famous Capybaras

Popcorn and Marshmallow, a pair of capybaras, were awarded the prestigious "Best Animal Duo" prize at a ceremony. Their chemistry and charm captured the hearts of both the judges and the audience.

Coco and Gucci, two capybaras, were the stars of an advertising campaign for a luxury brand. Their elegance and style were showcased in renowned fashion magazines.

Noodle and Ramen, two capybaras, were featured as the main characters in a children's animated series. Their amusing and educational escapades were shown in multiple countries across the globe.

Famous Capybaras

Apple and Cinnamon, two capybaras, were the heroes of a successful comic book. Their captivating adventures and positive values inspired many readers.

Princess and Prince, two capybaras, were the models for several famous paintings. Their beauty and grace inspired many talented artists.

Cupcake and Cookie, two capybaras, were the spokespeople for a campaign to raise awareness about protecting endangered animals. Their adorable image and touching story encouraged individuals to take action to safeguard these species.

Famous Capybaras

Licorice and Chocolate, two capybaras, were the stars of an eco-friendly circus show. Their talent for acrobatic acts was showcased in an environmentally conscious setting.

Harmony and Zen, two capybaras, were the icons of a wellness product brand. Their serenity and love for nature were used to promote a balanced lifestyle.

Tango and Serenade, a pair of capybaras, were featured in an acclaimed wildlife documentary. Their captivating tale enthralled audiences around the globe.

Famous Capybaras

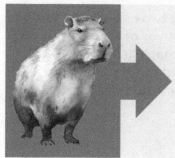

Cookie and Cream, two capybaras, were featured as special guests on a culinary television show, bringing joy to renowned chefs with their gourmet presence and passion for gastronomy.

Chérie and Amour, two capybaras, served as the official mascots of a famous wildlife park. Their gentleness and interaction with visitors made them favorites among the public.

Truffle and Mustache, a pair of capybaras, starred in a wildlife documentary series, where their intriguing lifestyle and natural habitat were extensively examined in every episode.

Famous Capybaras

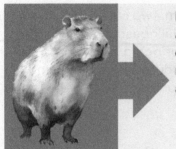

Fleur and Papillon, two capybaras, served as the representatives of a reforestation campaign. Their image in harmony with nature encouraged people to plant trees and preserve the environment.

Nougat and Caramel, two capybaras, were the protagonists of a popular video game. Their virtual adventures and charm captivated players worldwide.

Caramel and Chantilly, two capybaras, were the stars of an educational video series about animals. Their behavior and characteristics were explained in a playful manner to the viewers.

CAPYBARAS AND COMMUNICATION

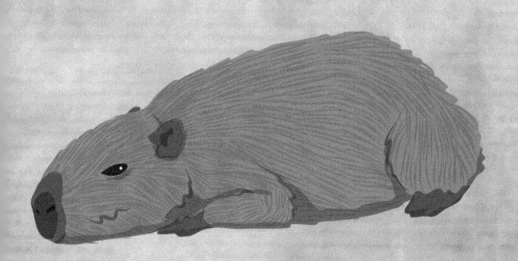

Capybaras and Communication

Capybaras are highly social creatures that live in communities known as herds. They engage in social interactions to maintain group harmony and support each other in foraging and protecting against predators.

Capybaras utilize a variety of vocalizations to communicate, emitting whistles to warn other members of the herd about danger, thereby creating a highly efficient alert communication system.

Moreover, capybaras employ visual cues for communication as well. For example, they might lick the noses of fellow group members to demonstrate affection and submission.

Capybaras and Communication

 Capybaras display social grooming behavior, coming together in groups to groom each other, keeping their fur clean and healthy. This behavior also reinforces social bonds within the herd.

 Additionally, capybaras utilize scent marking as a form of communication, having specialized glands that secrete pheromones to demarcate territory and convey information regarding their social status.

 In times of danger, capybaras emit sharp whistles to alert other herd members, allowing them to protect themselves and avoid potential predators.

25

Capybaras and Communication

 Capybaras have a great ability to recognize members of their group. They can distinguish them by their scent and distinctive physical characteristics, which facilitates communication and social interactions.

 Capybaras use their body posture to communicate. For example, when they stand up with their fur raised on their backs, it may indicate that they feel threatened or are seeking to assert dominance.

 Capybaras also use facial expressions to communicate. For instance, when they are relaxed, they have half-closed eyes and a gentle expression, whereas when they are angry or stressed, their eyes widen, and they show their teeth.

Capybaras and Communication

Capybaras demonstrate collective alarm behavior. When one member of the group senses danger, it emits a warning call, promptly alerting the rest of the herd, allowing them to respond swiftly and find safety.

Capybaras use facial expressions to communicate. For example, when they are relaxed, they have half-closed eyes and a gentle expression, whereas when they are angry or stressed, their eyes widen, and they show their teeth.

Capybaras, being semi-aquatic creatures, spend a considerable amount of time in water, which allows them to communicate with other group members using visual signals, such as body movements in the water.

Capybaras and Communication

Baby capybaras make soft chirping noises to call their mother. Cuddled up to her, they communicate extensively to form strong emotional bonds.

To intimidate a rival, the male capybara growls and shows its teeth. It also raises the fur on its back to appear larger!

The capybara employs body language by lifting its tail or fur to convey its feelings and states of mind.

Capybaras and Communication

Capybaras frequently sleep nestled close to one another, showcasing their affection and mutual trust through their physical proximity!

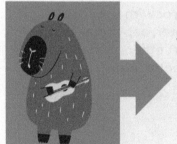

The capybara possesses a scent gland just above its nose that secretes a substance for marking its environment and communicating its presence to other capybaras.

As excellent swimmers, the capybara uses sounds and its webbed feet to stay in touch with other members of its group when moving through waterways and marshes.

Capybaras and Communication

Capybaras, highly social animals, enjoy cuddling up against each other when they sleep, eat, groom, or bask in the sun. This physical closeness demonstrates their mutual affection and strengthens their social bonds.

Even while eating or with their heads submerged in water, capybaras can emit alarm calls to alert others of danger while continuing their activities!

Even though they don't make noise, a baby capybara can recognize its mother's scent and differentiate her call to always stay in communication with her when necessary.

Capybaras and Communication

Even as adults, the capybara continues to squeak and chirp like a baby! These high-pitched sounds actually serve to strengthen bonds within the group and to request attention.

To warn of danger, the capybara strikes the ground with its feet. This visual signal quickly alerts other group members of a possible risk.

Baby capybaras are born with an amazing instinct: to communicate when they are cold! By huddling together, they raise their body temperature.

Capybaras and Communication

The capybara uses the loud clacking of its jaws to express positive emotions such as joy, entertainment, or excitement. It's a simple way to communicate messages!

Beware anyone who gets too close to the baby capybara! Its mother may growl, show teeth, or even lunge to protect her offspring and drive away the intruder.

The capybara enjoys bathing in mud not only to protect itself from the sun but also to communicate its presence and leave olfactory signals to other members of its group.

Capybaras and Communication

When they feel safe, capybaras cuddle up to each other to sleep. This physical closeness allows them to communicate in a tactile and comforting way.

Capybaras make sounds that are too low-pitched for humans to hear! However, they use these infrasounds to communicate across long distances.

According to a Native American legend, the capybara is renowned for its ability to master the secret language of the forest. That's why all the other animals respect it so much!

Capybaras and Communication

 The baby capybara can swim and even dive without learning! Its swimming abilities allow it to communicate with its mother underwater.

 Some wild capybaras are capable of understanding and responding to the whistles of shepherds. It's an amazing inter-species collaboration!

 The capybara is proficient in animal communication, capable of emitting ultrasonic sounds or utilizing ground vibrations to effectively convey messages!

Capybaras and Communication

The capybara employs a range of body positions, utilizing its fur, ears, tail, and teeth, to visually convey its intentions to fellow group members.

Capybaras, which are highly empathetic animals, can console members of their group by licking or cuddling with them when they are stressed or sick.

Capybaras exhibit strong empathy and can provide solace to members of their group by licking or snuggling with them when they are feeling stressed or unwell.

THE HABITAT OF CAPYBARAS

The Habitat of Capybaras

 The capybara uses its paws to create pathways through the marsh vegetation, making it easier to navigate. These channels make its habitat look like an aquatic maze!

 The capybara always rolls in the mud before entering the water. As it dries, this mud forms a natural sun protection on its bare and sensitive skin.

 Although excellent swimmers, capybaras never venture into the open sea. They always stay close to the mainland and the banks that constitute their preferred territories.

The Habitat of Capybaras

To regulate its body temperature, the capybara looks for cool spots during the hot hours of the day. It may be seen resting in muddy puddles or under the dense shade of vegetation.

The capybara can survive for a certain period in salty waters. Its widespread distribution demonstrates its ability to adapt to various aquatic environments.

Sometimes, the capybara digs its burrow under elevated tree roots, sheltered from terrestrial predators and sudden floods. A secure secondary habitat for it and its family!

The Habitat of Capybaras

Capybaras commonly sleep in shelters located near water, such as dense bushes or tree stumps. Some may also opt for burrows they've either dug themselves or reused.

Territorial animals, they live in groups of about twenty individuals and mark their territory with scent glands. Their territory can cover between 10 and 20 hectares centered around their water source.

Baby capybaras are typically born on land, often in proximity to water. At birth, they weigh around 1 to 1.5 kg! Soon after, they begin to trail their parents and acquire the skill of swimming.

The Habitat of Capybaras

Capybaras are particularly drawn to tropical and subtropical wetlands, which are abundant in South America. They can be observed from Panama to Argentina.

In certain habitats, capybara populations can reach very high densities near water sources. It's not uncommon for a hundred individuals to share the same pond!

If capybaras live near humans, they may sometimes venture into cultivated fields or gardens to feed, mainly during the night.

The Habitat of Capybaras

 Despite their excellent swimming ability, capybaras are not great divers. They tend to dive only for feeding or escaping a predator, and they generally stay near the surface.

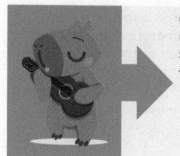 Capybaras find refuge in dense bushes, under stumps, or in holes along the banks. Some may even rest on lily pads or other floating aquatic plants!

 The brownish-red fur of capybaras offers superb camouflage in the marshes filled with vegetation where they make their home.

The Habitat of Capybaras

 Capybaras tend to come out primarily at dusk or at night to feed in the meadows. They are more active early in the morning and late in the day when temperatures are cooler.

 When food is scarce, capybaras can travel up to 6 kilometers round trip each night between their water source and grazing areas.

 During the rainy season, capybaras have access to larger territories and more food. Groups are then less concentrated around water sources.

The Habitat of Capybaras

 The deeper the water, the better it is for capybaras! This provides them with a safe refuge from land predators like pumas that cannot follow them there.

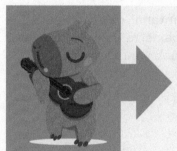 The larger and more vegetation-rich the capybaras' territory is, the better it is for them! This ensures an ample food supply for the entire group.

 When resting or sleeping, capybaras often adopt positions that allow for maximum vigilance against potential dangers.

The Habitat of Capybaras

Capybaras are often found near water points overrun by water hyacinths. Its long roots provide them with excellent refuge.

In the Brazilian Pantanal, capybaras are abundant in the baías, marshy plains that partially dry up each year.

In the Iguaçu area, which straddles the border of Argentina and Brazil, numerous capybaras inhabit the banks of the Rio Paraná and its calmer tributaries.

The Habitat of Capybaras

During the dry season, capybaras gather around the last remaining waterholes. Population density can become very high.

The disappearance of wetlands in Central and Northern Brazil endangers the future of several isolated capybara populations.

The main long-term threats to many wild capybara populations are deforestation and the depletion of wetlands.

CAPYBARAS
AND PLANTS

Capybaras and Plants

Capybaras are herbivores that exclusively feed on plants. They graze on numerous species of grasses, aquatic plants, barks, or fruits found in their habitat. Their diet is very diverse.

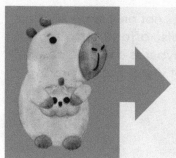

In wetland areas, capybaras particularly enjoy edible bulrushes and broad-leaved cattails. These aquatic plants play a significant role in their daily diet.

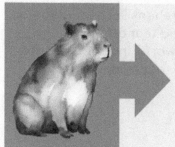

Capybaras consume various types of grasses such as ryegrasses, panic grasses, or barnyard grasses. These prairie grasses also serve as a staple food.

Capybaras and Plants

Capybaras dedicate 5 to 8 hours daily to eating. During the remaining time, they either ruminate over their food or soak up the sun. Feeding constitutes their primary activity!

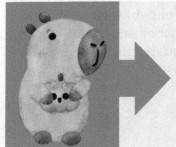

The aquatic plants not only serve as their food source but also offer them a secure hiding place. Capybaras can hide beneath the wide leaves of water lilies or among roots.

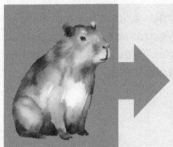

Thanks to their prehensile lips, capybaras can easily grab and tear off plants and grasses. Their powerful incisor teeth cut through even the toughest stems.

Capybaras and Plants

Capybaras prefer to feed early in the morning or late in the evening when temperatures are lower. They are more active at dusk or during the night.

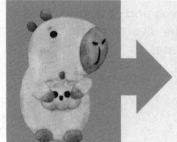

Capybaras prefer to feed early in the morning or late in the evening when temperatures are cooler. The rest of the time, they ruminate while lying in the shade.

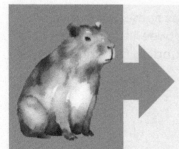

Capybaras also consume fallen fruits from trees growing along the water's edge, such as guavas, palm fruits, or figs.

Capybaras and Plants

During the dry season, when plants become scarce, capybaras have to eat more bark, fruits, or roots to survive.

Sweet potato leaves and cassava stems are also among the diverse foods that capybaras consume.

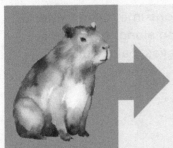

To feed, capybaras sometimes cover long distances between their water source and surrounding feeding areas.

Capybaras and Plants

 Thanks to their powerful jaws, capybaras can easily crush most plants, even tough or thorny ones. Their molars are also well adapted for grinding.

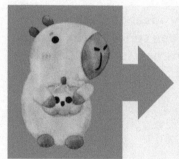 While capybaras are mainly herbivores, they occasionally add small aquatic invertebrates like snails or insects to their diet.

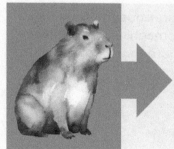 During the dry season, the absence of green vegetation can weaken capybaras, leaving them more susceptible to diseases and predators.

Capybaras and Plants

Young capybaras learn to recognize edible plants by imitating their parents, enabling them to find the best food sources.

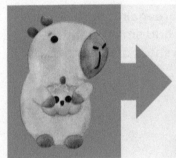

Due to their highly advanced sense of smell, capybaras can sense the existence of edible plants from as far as 200 meters away.

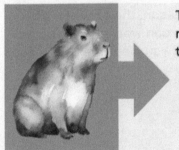

To survive, capybaras need to feed regularly. Their stomachs do not allow them to fast for more than a few hours.

Capybaras and Plants

The teeth of capybaras continuously grow to compensate for the wear caused by their abrasive plant-based diet. They wear down by about 5 cm per year.

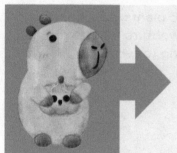

Capybaras, which live near the forests along rivers in South America, occasionally delight in munching on young bamboo shoots.

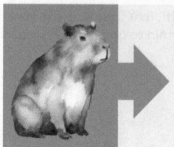

Capybaras consume a diverse range of fern species found in the wetlands of South America.

Capybaras and Plants

When water becomes scarce in the dry season, capybaras have to travel long distances to find green food.

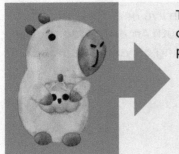

To access aquatic plants, capybaras don't hesitate to venture far into the ponds, even having to swim.

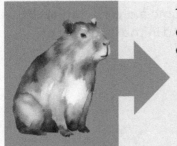

Thanks to their efficient liver, capybaras can consume certain toxic plants in small quantities.

CAPYBARAS AND THEIR BEHAVIOR

Capybaras and Their Behavior

Capybaras are social creatures that form groups of up to fifty individuals. They enjoy the company of others and value close bonds within their community.

Capybaras have a rather sedentary lifestyle. They spend their lives near their water source and territory, which they know perfectly well.

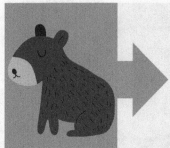

Although they have a clumsy appearance, capybaras can run fast and swim agilely. However, they prefer to take it slow and enjoy their time.

Capybaras and Their Behavior

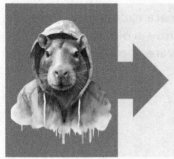

Capybaras are typically tranquil and gentle creatures. Nevertheless, dominant males might engage in battles to assert their dominance over one another.

Capybaras, being social creatures, often sleep huddled together, which also helps them share body warmth.

When danger is nearby, the capybara emits a barking sound as an alert to its companions, signaling them to flee.

Capybaras and Their Behavior

Even though they are excellent swimmers, capybaras prudently avoid venturing into deep or choppy waters, preferring to stay near the shores.

Female capybaras have a strong maternal instinct and may behave aggressively to shield their young from potential dangers. They are prompt in assuming a leadership role in warding off threats.

Capybaras typically sleep for around 4 to 5 hours each day. The rest of their time is spent eating, grooming, and staying alert to their surroundings.

Capybaras and Their Behavior

 Young capybaras are very playful and enjoy spending hours chasing each other, engaging in friendly fights, or swimming together.

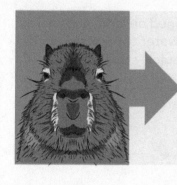 Capybaras have a remarkable sense of direction and exceptional spatial memory, allowing them to be thoroughly familiar with their natural environment.

 Although gregarious, capybaras also enjoy occasionally isolating themselves from the group to rest quietly without being disturbed.

Capybaras and Their Behavior

 Capybaras often rub against objects or roll in the mud to mark their territory with their scent.

 If they feel threatened on land, capybaras dash towards the water to seek refuge in haste. They swim quickly and adeptly.

 If capybaras are disturbed during their rest, they emit a warning grunt to show their displeasure.

Capybaras and Their Behavior

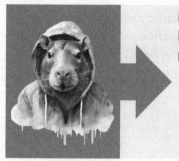

Frequent disturbance by humans can lead capybaras to become nocturnal as a protective measure.

Capybaras have very keen hearing. They detect the slightest suspicious noise and immediately become alert.

Capybaras often adopt strange positions for sleeping, resting their heads on the body of another individual.

Capybaras and Their Behavior

Capybaras also communicate through touch, by rubbing their noses together or giving friendly little head bumps.

Although playful and affectionate with each other, capybaras remain wary and fearful of humans and strangers.

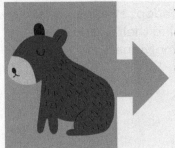

Young male capybaras typically leave their original social group around the age of 2 and then lead a solitary life, often exploring new areas.

Capybaras and Their Behavior

Capybaras do not hesitate to bite when they feel threatened. Their powerful jaws are capable of inflicting serious injuries.

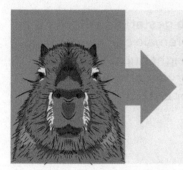

In the presence of a terrestrial predator, capybaras may sometimes assume a defensive posture, lowering their heads and showing their teeth.

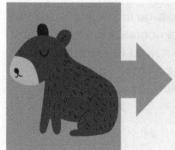

Capybaras sleep with their eyes half-closed and are generally more in a state of drowsiness than deep sleep. They always remain alert.

Capybaras and Their Behavior

Capybaras can stay underwater for up to five minutes to escape predators. They use this technique to hide from jaguars and caimans. It's an excellent survival strategy.

Capybaras have a gestation period of five months. The female can give birth to a litter of one to eight pups. Young capybaras are very precocious and can swim shortly after birth.

Capybaras seek refuge in the water while also utilizing it as a socializing space. They engage in play, rest, and feeding activities in aquatic habitats. Water constitutes the essence of their daily existence.

Capybaras and Their Behavior

Their hind legs are slightly longer than their front legs. This characteristic gives them a distinctive gait, which is useful both on land and in water.

Despite their large size, capybaras can effectively conceal themselves in tall grass. They employ this tactic to evade predators.

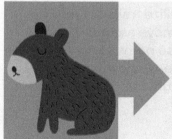

In the dry season, they might excavate the soil to locate moisture, showcasing their adaptability to shifting conditions. They exhibit great resourcefulness in their strategies for survival.

Capybaras and Their Behavior

Capybaras have a unique method for regulating their body heat. They can increase blood flow to their skin to cool down, helping them tolerate high temperatures.

Capybaras contribute significantly to seed dispersal by ingesting fruits and carrying seeds to different locations, which aids in habitat regeneration and underscores their vital role in ecological balance.

Capybaras can utilize trails created by other animals to move around. They take advantage of these paths to access water or new grazing areas, showing their opportunistic nature.

CAPYBARAS AND MYTHS

Capybaras and Myths

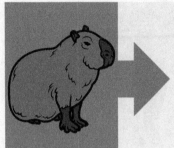 In certain South American communities, the sighting of a capybara is viewed as a harbinger of forthcoming heavy rains. This creature is intimately connected with water.

 In Brazilian popular culture, the capybara is often associated with an image of tranquility and serenity. It is regarded as a symbol of inner peace.

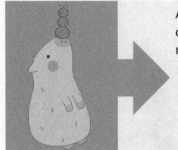 Amazonian Indians tell a story that the creator made the capybara the king of all rodents because of its imposing size.

Capybaras and Myths

 According to a Guarani legend, the god Tupã transformed a disobedient child into a capybara to teach him humility.

 In Amazonian shamanism, there's a belief that the capybara possesses supernatural powers such as foreseeing the future or healing illnesses.

 Amazonian Indians say that the capybara has a wise spirit because it always prefers fleeing to confrontation.

Capybaras and Myths

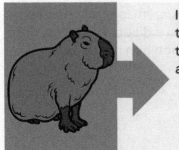 In the legends of the Amazon, it is said that the capybara was born from the transformation of a young girl into an animal, due to the jealousy of a shaman.

 The Wayampi Indians believe that the capybara's spirit guards water sources and punishes those who contaminate or waste this sacred resource.

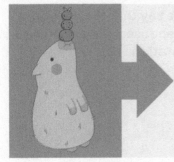 According to the beliefs of the Piaroa communities, the capybara holds the secret of immortality but only reveals it to the wisest.

Capybaras and Myths

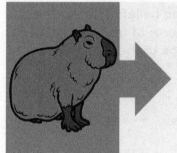

As per a Tukano legend, encountering the gaze of a capybara during daylight is linked with misfortune, whereas at night it signals a time of prosperity.

Mapuche shamans believe that the spirit of the capybara teaches them patience and wisdom during their visions.

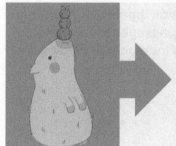

According to some shamans, dreaming of a capybara is interpreted as a sign of fertile rains to come after a period of drought.

Capybaras and Myths

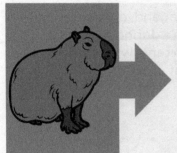

According to Taino beliefs, the capybara possesses the secret of medicinal plants and leads shamans to their healing properties.

According to some Guarani legends, the creator bestowed upon the capybara the ability to walk on water as a reward for its wisdom.

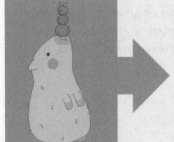

According to an Inca legend, the capybara showed a secret passage through the Andes to help the Inca people escape their enemies.

Capybaras and Myths

The Ayoreo Indians hold the belief that the capybara's kind spirit safeguards water sources and penalizes those who contaminate or squander them.

According to the Guaranis, the capybara teaches humans the art of peacefully resolving conflicts through its conciliatory behavior.

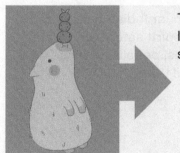

The Machiguengas see the gregarious lifestyle of the capybara as an example of social harmony and community solidarity.

Capybaras and Myths

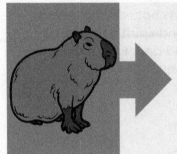

The Piaroas believe that the capybara holds the secret of immortality but shares it only with the wisest and most nature-respecting individuals.

The Guarani legend tells of the capybara being born from the transformation of a mischievous child into an animal, aiming to impart wisdom.

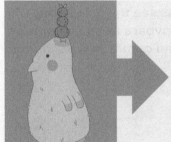

According to Achuar Indian beliefs, the capybara's kind spirit safeguards water sources and areas, penalizing those who pollute or despoil them.

Capybaras and Myths

As per the beliefs of the Atacamas in Chile, the wisdom and insight of the capybara's spirit inspired shamans and leaders of clans.

To the Tainos, observing a capybara close to a water spring was interpreted as an indication of protective spirits watching over that sacred spring.

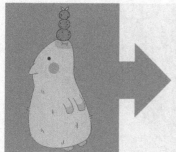

According to the Mapuches, the capybara held the secret of medicinal plants in the forest and passed it on to shamans in their dreams.

CAPYBARAS AND HUMANS

Capybaras and Humans

Capybaras are very sociable animals and enjoy the company of humans. They are often described as affectionate and docile pets.

In Venezuela, it is a tradition to adopt a baby capybara as a pet. Raised on a bottle and then weaned, the capybara follows its owner everywhere in the house and gets along well with other pets.

Capybaras are smart animals that learn to recognize their names and respond to simple commands rapidly. With patience, they can be trained to walk on a leash, shake hands, and even perform tricks!

Capybaras and Humans

Despite their imposing size, capybaras are not aggressive towards humans in their natural environment. They simply observe them from a distance or flee if they feel threatened.

In some cities, one can observe wild capybaras strolling through parks and gardens in search of food. Although this may be surprising at first, residents eventually become accustomed to their calm and peaceful presence.

Certain spas in Japan and Russia utilize capybaras as therapy animals, believing that interacting with these calming rodents can help alleviate stress and anxiety in humans.

Capybaras and Humans

Trained capybaras are occasionally featured in movies, television series, and advertisements because of their cute and harmless demeanor. They can be easily directed on a film set.

In zoos, capybara enclosures allow the public to get close and observe these calm and sociable animals up close. Children love watching them lounging around or splashing in the water.

Capybaras are sensitive to loud noises and stressful environments, making their maintenance challenging in zoos that are heavily frequented by the public.

Capybaras and Humans

 Trained capybaras recognize their owner and loudly express their joy when they return home after an absence.

 Capybaras must always live in groups to be happy. Separated from their peers, they wither away and exhibit self-destructive behavior.

 Capybaras are excellent swimmers thanks to their webbed feet. In some water parks in South America, it is possible to swim with these fascinating animals.

82

83

84

85

86

Made in the USA
Las Vegas, NV
01 May 2024

89381319R00049